CHiPS

Poems
by
Jim Rapp

Copyright
November, 2014
by James D. Rapp
All rights reserved
ISBN 13: 978-0-9828507-9-4

To
Kylie and Aidan
A Prayer

Kylie and Aidan are the most recent "chips" to fly off the old block. May their world be to them a place of wonder, of opportunity, and of accomplishment. May they be sustained by a faith in the God and Father of our Lord Jesus Christ as their Grandmother and I have been. May they pass on to their children and grandchildren that eternal faith, undiminished by the ever-changing world in which they all will live.

The Chipmeister

The last real house in which Alice and I lived was one that I "built myself." Now, anyone who knows me well knows that I could not build a modern house by myself, and I didn't. Two capable friends – Wayne Beard, who knew how to read and execute blueprints, and Steve Velie, whose strength was called upon at strategic times – were hired to do that which I was neither trained, nor capable of doing. And several other friends and relatives chipped in to help bring the project to perfection.

My part was not insignificant – I want that known, of course – but a significant part of my job was keeping the place cleared of debris so that we could work safely. At the end of each day I would sweep up the clutter of broken sheetrock and board ends that had accumulated, sort through it to retrieve anything useable and deposit the rest in a dumpster to be hauled away to the city landfill.

The lot upon which we built the house was populated, before we began our project, with more than sixty trees, the majority of them pines with a diameter of ten to fifteen inches, but four or five were aged hard maples measuring twenty or more inches in diameter. All of those trees were cut into firewood lengths and corded up to be split for burning in our fireplace.

That, too, was a chore that fell to me when I had "nothing better" to be working on. I soon discovered that, at age 62, after a "dissolute life" of leisure (teaching), I no longer had the strength to split that much wood. One day a young farm lad, whom Wayne had brought along as a helper, asked if I'd like to have him split some wood during the times he had nothing else to do. What a demonstration of wood-splitting he gave us. In just a handful of hours I had a shed-full of winter fuel and only a small pile of "stubborn stumps" that would require splitting by a mechanical splitter.

Needless to say, there were thousands of chips and splinters too small to be useful even as kindling. Again it fell to me to rake them up and dispose of them, either by burning them or bagging them up to be hauled away to the landfill.

So I have become something of an expert in dealing with miscellanea, a chipmeister perhaps. I do know how to bag up useless chips and send them off to landfills. But I have always found it hard to do so without retrieving that which I felt was useful, some of the bigger chips.

I have found that my poems are often constructed from the "chips" that are left from a day of working with more holistic ideas. The mundane and the necessary fills my thoughts most of the time; I split it, and pile it, and assume that it will meet the needs for which it is being processed. It is the "main thing" that I'm doing. Or at least I feel that it is.

But what to do with the pesky chips that keep piling up: the ideas that popped into my head prompting me to make a note of them; that fragment of thought that has nagged me for weeks, or even years; the persistent notion that I thought I had sent off to the landfill long ago but it never seems to go away; the urgent call to speak out on an idea or action that I feel is contrary to good sense; the desire to brighten someone's day with some words of encouragement? On and on the chips keep coming. What to do with them?

Obviously I've decided that they are too valuable to discard. They may not be suitable for use in "building a house." But a splinter could be used to start a fire. Some small blocks might challenge the imagination of a child. And more substantial chips may be useful in a project.

What follows is a collection of chips. I offer them as my contribution to the conservation of ideas, hoping others will find use for them.

I have also chosen to utilize the otherwise unused spaces in the book to feature some of the other "chips" in our lives besides Kylie and Aidan to whom this volume is dedicated. Each child and grandchild is poem unto herself or himself. The photos are presented, unlabeled, to give deniability to the subjects if they wish to remain anonymous. Each chip is a treasure to their grandmother and I. It seems our lives could not have been complete without them.

Solomon warned his "son" that, "the writing of many books is endless, and excessive devotion to books is wearying to the body." How true. And the editing of those books is potentially just as endless; each new pass through reveals another error to correct. To the degree that this volume is "error-free" the credit goes largely to my dear wife of fifty-seven years. Alice's ability to ferret out a missing word, a misspelling, a malapropism, or any other fault is uncanny. Of course she should bear no responsibility for any errors not yet expunged; it was I, after all, who put them there.

Contents

Vegewels – Poems of Whimsy ... 1

An Author's Dilemma ... 3
Gallup-in In Circles ... 3
kids again (a haiku quartet) ... 4
zephered ... 4
A Business Note ... 5
Touched by An Angel In A Shirt Too Small ... 5
Vegewels ... 7
Oh Shucks! ... 7
A Rare Correction ... 8
Too Much Self-examination ... 8
Advent of the Promise Drone ... 9
Single Snowflake Threatens Millions ... 11
Elucidate ... 12
Not News ... 12
Sliding Into Heaven ... 13
Responding to an NYT Report ... 13
We're (Not) Using Our Heads ... 14
Working The Night Shift ... 15

Sharing a Treat – Poems of Love and Friendship ... 17

Extending Love ... 19
Son time on a Rainy Day: November 6, 2013 ... 19

A Subtle Word 20
Your You-ness 21
That You Are There 21
Shared Endeavors – Shared Rewards 22
Sharing 23
Coupled 23
No Ordinary Cloth 24
Body Lovers 24
Doggy Kisses 25
Sharing A Treat 25

A Day When Stones Cried Out – Remembrance 27

A Haiku for Lola 29
Sunday Afternoons of Old 29
An Old-fashioned Christmas Card 32
A Day When Stones Cried Out 33
Arizona Tragedy (A Haiku) 33
An *ism* With A Father's Heart 34

When I Am Gone – The Art of Writing 35

Inbreathed (A Haiku) 37
Making Do With What I Have 37
A Two-line Poem 38
When I am Gone 38
Adjectives Are For Poets . . . Uh, Poor Poets 40
Wrecking Your Chances 40

The Value of a Dream – Poems About Fairie 41

Shadows 43
Legions of Darkness 44
Firiel 46
Galadriel 47
Morning in a Fairie Glen 48
The Value of a Dream 48
To Fairie and Back on a Foggy Morning 48
Sun-dappled Days 58

Spider Lives – Prophetic Poems 59

Watching an Old Man Outlive His Wisdom 61
The Prophet in the Wilderness – Marilynne Robinson 61
Week-end Fare 63
A Long Journey Back to Where We Began –
    Hanging our Thoughts on a Vapor 63
Justice, Blind Justice (A Haiku Quartet) 65
The Human Malady 66
Standing Watch: Questions for an Ancient Tree
    In a Chicago Park 67
Mikhail Kalashnikov, How Do I Love Thee? 69
Grieving the Uses of BG 71
Believe Me, We Are Awash In Anonymity –
    Seven Haiku for Anonymity 72
The Righting of the Costa Concordia 73

Perverting a Good Thing 74
Bucking the Lord's Day 75
Against Blind Intolerance of Islam 75
Aerial Warfare (A Haiku Trio) 76
Spider Lives 77
Don't Forget to Send in the Cash 79
And They Say The Taxes Are Eating Us Alive 79
Praying for Nero 80
Hand-me-down Warfare – A Meditation from a
    Lover of Fireworks 81

The Cost of a Burger – Just Thinkin' Out Loud 83

Thank God for Words 85
Should I Join Facebook? 86
The Hurt and the Hurter (A Haiku Meditation) 87
Let There Be Light (A Haiku Quartet) 88
What is the Cost of a Burger? 89
Who Is My Friend? 90
Things Missed and Things Missed 90
The High Price of Ageing (A Haiku Lament) 92
Our Final Resting Place (Haiku Musings) 93
Shredding (1952 – 2014) 94

A Borning Light – Poems of Faith 97

Treasures in Earthen Vessels 99
The Serpent in Eden (A Haiku Quartet) 99
This Day (A Haiku) 100
A Haiku for Sinners 100
Your Presence (A Haiku Trio) 100
Four (or Five) Haiku Proverbs 101
An Easter Haiku 102
A Borning Light 102
Simple Faith (A Haiku) 103
A (Haiku) Gospel Quartet 103
résumé 104
Fall Colors Make Me Believe 105
An Old Man's Dilemma (A Haiku) 105
He Comes (A Haiku Quartet) 106
No Shame In Going Home 106
Substantial Evidence (Haiku Structure) 107
Spread the Joy 108
Though You Make Your Bed In Hell 109
Unseen Presence 111
Two Poor Rich Men 112

To Everything A Season – Poems Celebrating Nature 115

A Rainy July Morning (A Haiku Trio) 117
A Cold Assize 117
An Ode To A Beautiful Wood 118
The Fall Guy 119
June 30th In Wisconsin 119
A Haiku for Luna 120
spring thaw (a haiku) 121
A Golden Blossom Frond 121
April Snowstorm 122
An Overblown Storm 122
To Everything A Season 123
Jack Frost 123
Golden Bird 124

Alphabetical List of Poems 127
About the Author 133

Vegewels
Poems of Whimsy

One of Harry Belafonte's simplest songs is also one with beautiful lyrics, *I'm Just A Country Boy*. The song relates the feelings of a poor boy who is in love with a beautiful girl whom he knows he can never win. So he contents himself 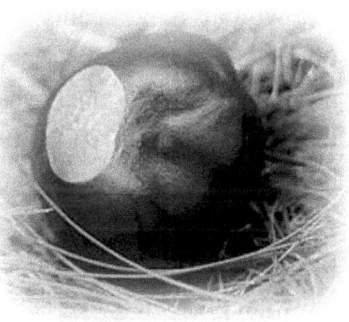 with the treasures a poor boy has – "silver in the stars, and gold in the morning sun."

Being a poor boy, as were all the boys I knew, but nonetheless wishing to impress and win the heart of the pretty daughter of the Presbyterian minister, I had to improvise. I was not as resigned to my fate as was Harry Belafonte's country boy. The stars were beyond my reach and the sun too hot to handle, so I seized upon the nearest thing at hand, a buckeye, the fruit of the horse chestnut – *Aesculus hippocastanum* – tree.

The buckeye is an extraordinarily beautiful fruit. Its hard shell of deep, dark, lustrous brown, surrounds the lighter, tan "eye". It rivaled even a pen knife as a treasure for a young boy to carry in his pocket. So I could think of nothing better with

Vegewels: Poems of Whimsy

which to fashion a heart-winning gift for the girl of my dreams.

My father, a deeply sentimental man who, in his youth wooed and won a young beauty who became my mother, understood my need and became my accomplice in drilling holes in a number of choice buckeyes and threading them on a simple length of string, saved from a package of ground meat brought home from the butcher's shop.

If Cynthia was disappointed in the vegetarian treasure with which I presented her, she did not show it. I am sure it no longer exists, perhaps not even in her mind, but it may well have been the first "vegewel" (vegetable-jewel) ever conceived by the mind of a young man.

In the years that have ensued, my poverty has only deepened. The stars are even farther from my reach, the sun is certainly no cooler, still far too hot to touch, and I am too old to be making buckeye necklaces.

It is my hope that, in lieu of more tangible treasure, you will be as gracious as my first love and receive this gift of light-hearted literary vegewels.

Vegewels: Poems of Whimsy

An Author's Dilemma

It is better to remain silent
and thought to be a heretic
than to write a book
and provide the evidence.

⸻

With apologies to Anonymous

Gallup-ing In Circles

Gallup tells us what we think,
believe, or hope, or plan
and so that is what we think,
believe, and hope, and plan
so when Gallup asks us
what we think,
believe, and hope, and plan.
it is no surprise to read
that Gallup finds that this
is what we think,
believe, and hope and plan.

Vegewels: Poems of Whimsy

**kids again
(a haiku quartet)**

our teacher gave us
flower seeds to plant today;
are we kids again?

all over fifty
yet we'll do as we are told;
'cuz we're kids again.

we will plant the seeds,
watch them grow, and be amazed
like we're kids again.

parables unfold
as each seed sprouts and teaches
God's old kids again

zephyred

scrapping its pledge of
silent anonymity –
airing my secret

Vegewels: Poems of Whimsy

A Business Note
(About the opening underscore for *The Promise*)

I've mixed the family lines with the overture
And though I'd have to say I'm not over sure,
I think the mix will do the job for us.
That's all, from the old theater cat, Gus.

Touched By An Angel In A Shirt Too Small

He had a perpetually un-telling smile,
a shirt buttoned top and bottom,
two buttons each and all the while
he stood as though accustomed
to the company he sought to join.

An angel unawares?
With belly shining though?
He seemed not at all to care
that no one present knew
he wished, our group to join.

When asked if he had come
to be a part of our three-tabled band
– as if to make himself at home –
he smilingly (unspeakingly) sought a place to land;
not too good (apparently) a clan like ours to join.

Vegewels: Poems of Whimsy

Once seated his tongue was freed;
And H, whom rumor has it, had invited him,
became the target of his screed;
poor H could hardly get a sentence in;
our "angel" kept a one-way conversation going.

Though most had finished their eggs or cakes
he caught up soon; "Two eggs over hard, please."
The whites separated and downed in one take;
the yolks smothered in catsup, each a double squeeze;
two gulps each – they never knew where they were going.

"Be careful to entertain strangers," we're told;
"In so doing some have entertained angels unawares."
He may be one – an angel, I mean – but if so I make bold,
in light of his dress, demeanor, and mystic smile, to declare
him one of the strangest strangers that heaven has going.

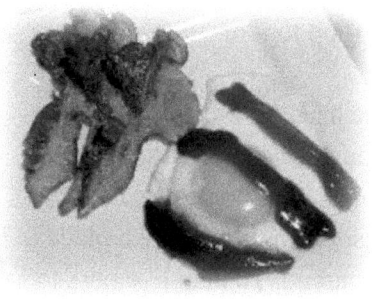

Vegewels: Poems of Whimsy

Vegewels

To some folks I know,
A buckeye is a mere horse chestnut,
Which only goes to show
The culture they've not got yet.

A buckeye is a rare vegewel
That, when sent to one you love,
Perhaps strung on a lovely crewel,
Says, "You're the one I'm thinking of."

Oh Shucks!

When God said, "Let There Be!"
Matter rushed so quick to *be*
that all the universe became a sea
of clay the likes of you and me.

"Shucks!" said God, "Now how can we
make this swirling clayey sea
reveal, reflectively,
the Triune Face of We?"

Vegewels: Poems of Whimsy

Then spoke a voice so wee,
a clod from farthest far eternity:
"Master, though besmudged we be,
we'd like to show the likes of Thee."

A Rare Correction

The "suggested approach" you credit to me,
Was "suggested" by you, originally,
So take a sweet bow and half of the credit,
It won't go to your head unless you let it.

Too Much Self-examination

Jose was a fool as everyone knows
obsessively checking the state of his toes;
to assist in assessing his digits down low,
he walked barefooted, in the heat and the cold.

Vegewels: Poems of Whimsy

Advent of the Promised Drone

The prophet has spoken . . .

I heard just yesterday that drones
will soon deliver my Amazon
purchases – as soon as they have honed
the system. With all glitches gone,

at the FAA's approved hour,
the skies will be lighted by a million,
or a million to the hundredth candle power,
as mini semis, an Amazon battalion,

with no human hand to steer,
no human eye to see,
will descend and drop their gear
precisely where it's meant to be.

The prophecy is fulfilled . . .

Today I watched a "drone" in action,
pushing down our street a laden dolly,
piled high with boxes, often losing traction
on the icy sidewalk – losing boxes – what folly!

Vegewels: Poems of Whimsy

It was an auxiliary UPS delivery man.
On foot! Delivering – as postmen did of yore –
packages disgorged from a fleeing van
to be hand-delivered, from the dolly, door to door.

I wanted so to roll my window down –
human kindness alone deterred me –
and ask if he was the Promised Drone;
the Amazon Messiah that we seek.

Single Snowflake Threatens Millions

"Massive winter storm threatens up to 100 million in Midwest and Northeast"
(NBCNews.com headline, Jan 2, 2014)

The headline that greeted us this morning
is typical; there is no level of hype so intense,
no adjectival assemblage so suborning
as to make the weather persons wince.

Every weather front crossing west to east
"threatens" millions in its path
with summer heat or wintry sleet
that lingers as its aftermath.

The headline could read just as truthfully,
in letters bold enough to make us gasp,
**SINGLE SNOWFLAKE MENACINGLY
TARGETS MILLIONS IN ITS PATH!**

Vegewels: Poems of Whimsy

Elucidate

Confused, is what I am,
So help me if you can.
If you could just elucidate,
Then, with luck, I might relate.

**Not News
(A Haiku Quartet)**

Today we got some
"Not news". On days without news
we're given "Not news."

**"No private e-mail
system in the governor's
office."** *Headline news!*

Pseudo-news! No doubt
the newsroom is layered with
pseudo pseudo news

When nothing happens
print it. Pseudo happenings
are as good as gold

Vegewels: Poems of Whimsy

Sliding Into Heaven

He said, "I trust, by grace, I'll make it in."
"By grease?" she heard him say.
"Ah yes," he laughed, "I'll bring along a tin
of that – to slick the way."

Responding to an NYT Report
*(Mitt Romney ponders running
again for President of the U.S.)*

Mittens is sittin' in the midst of his gittin's
wonderin' if'n we've been forgittin',
wonderin' if'n it might be fittin'
if'n he'd run onest agin' 'stid a quittin'.
Ain't it all jist a bit side-splittin'?

Vegewels: Poems of Whimsy

We're (Not) Using Our Heads

Batters "beaned" by the ball,
Pitcher's felled by line drives,
Outfielders ramming the walls
Diving and risking their lives
Catcher and runner lie sprawled
Fans dancing and giving "high-fives"

Old "stars" wheeled through the halls
Arranged in neat rows by sixes and fives
Watch images move on the "walls" –
Observe bleakly with half-knowing eyes.
By now it should be obvious to all –
We're here for (not) using their heads, guys!

Someday Tiddlywinks teams –
Resourcefully using their heads –
Will make their game more "extreme"
By skull-banging the puck instead
So their widows can pitifully keen,
"He got Alzheimer's by (not) using his head."

Working the Night Shift

I hear talk of multi-tasking.
Younger minds, adept, and quick,
are good at it, contrasting
with old skulls grown thick.

But I have learned that even I,
ancient though I have become,
can stand my ground, even vie
with youth's quick metronome.

I've learned to work while sleeping!
Hah! Give that a try, you Punks.
I've typed five pages without peeping,
All perfect z's; a grand slam-dunk.

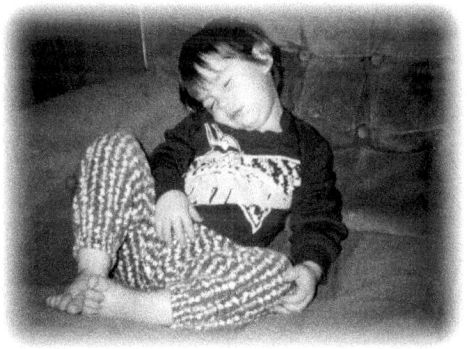

Vegewels: Poems of Whimsy

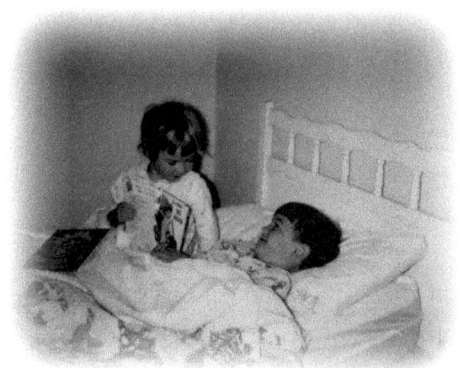

Sharing a Treat
Poems of Love and Friendship

Life without friendship is almost unimaginable. Perhaps that is the reason that friendship comes in so many shapes, sizes, colors and flavors. We must find a variety that suits us.

Cowboys sing of love for their horse. Country singers sing of love for a guitar. Children invent imaginary friends to fill the void when flesh and blood friends are not available. The elderly adopt a dog or cat and lavish on it all the love that is customary between human friends. Thieves fall in with thieves, politicians with politicians, saints with saints and sinners with sinners. There is an inextinguishable need in the human heart for friendship.

It would be interesting to know what percentage of all the songs the human race has created are devoted to either extolling love sought or love gained, or bemoaning love denied or love lost. Most of the memorable stories commemorate the deep love of friends. And, of course, the poet's pen has nearly drained the earth of ink in its attempt to describe the joys and heartaches associated with friendship.

Sharing A Treat: Poems of Love and Friendship

No number of poems would suffice to express love in all its many permutations. I offer here a mere dozen.

Sharing A Treat: Poems of Love and Friendship

Extending Love

A thousand words
from friend to friend
are just the way
that friends extend
the saying of what three
words will do – each word
conveying, "I love you."

**Son-time on a Rainy Day:
Nov. 6, 2013**

Rain is such a blessing,
bringing, if it comes,
two blessings I'm guessing;
son and perhaps grandson.

How old was I when, at last
I had a two-car attached garage?
At forty-six and aging fast
he's still chasing that mirage.

But for now he'll work in mine
on this cold and rainy day,
and, aging fast, we'll cherish the time;
make every precious minute pay.

A Subtle Word

"Apart" is such a subtle word –
Small imprinted, smaller heard –
But in the space its name suggests
A million aching wishes rest.

"A part" is such a healing thought –
By time and presence bought –
So e'en when two are far apart,
In all, they each can have a part.

Sharing A Treat: Poems of Love and Friendship

Your *Youness*

It is your *Youness* that we seek in you,
not *things* that wear away with age,
but the ordinary *things* you do
and say when you engage

on *friendship's* turf
with those you love;
the tiny little kerfs
you cut in hearts of

unsuspecting passersby,
made hard by daily living,
re-shaped by coming eye to eye
with *goodness* bent on unremitting giving.

That You Are There

That you are there,
a Morning Sun
to warm a waking world –
waking cold –
a Covert from the wind,
a Cottage on the Moor,
a Hand to reach to,

Sharing A Treat: Poems of Love and Friendship

an Arm to lean upon,
an over-eaving Beech Tree
giving shade
in which to rest,
a Dulcimer Song
that lifts my weary soul,
an Ayin Spring at which
to quench my thirst,
a Ruby Sunset
curtaining –
covering –
closing out
a day of heavy toil,
a Quieting Presence
in the darkness.

That you are there,
that you are there
is all I need to know.

Shared Endeavors – Shared Rewards

When two come alongside
To wrestle with a task or thought,
And, thus, the outcome, help decide,
Each owns an Ezer-share
    of what their efforts bought.

Sharing A Treat: Poems of Love and Friendship

Sharing

The wonderful thing about sharing one's treats
Is that it halves the calories and doubles the sweets.
It is that way with all the shared things that we do;
The pains are divided, the joys multiplied . . . times two.

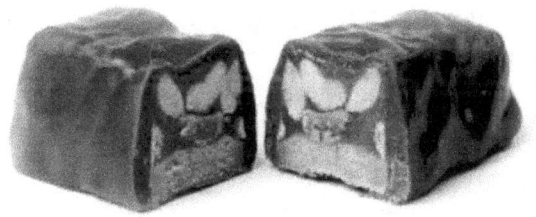

Coupled

Today she touched (and kissed) some things
he'd sacralized for her, and felt the strings
that bound their hearts tighten like the coupling
of two railroad cars; one implement that clings
relentlessly to two, securely linking,
in fixed relationship, the precious things
that every force but love is bent on weakening.

Sharing A Treat: Poems of Love and Friendship

No Ordinary Cloth

What is it about this piece of cloth,
that makes the old man take it off
the rack and wrap its fibers, soft,
around his face, as he does oft?

Is it *presence* he feels there;
the texture, mixed with scented air,
that brings a memory dear and rare;
a face and form once sweet and fair?

It's there he goes on lonely days,
when peace will come no other ways
and lifts the fibers to his waiting face,
to cure his aching heart's malaise.

Body Lovers

Body lovers make good friends;
    they overlook the body's "faults"
        because they love what is within.

Body lovers have no list of faults;
    each bulge and blight, bespeaking *friend*,
        becomes a treasure for love's vaults.

Doggy Kisses

When your neck is sore
And your brain's turned foggy
And your back can take no more,
Just whistle for your little doggy.

Running to his Mr. or his Missus,
Tail and tongue "in gear,"
Bearing friend-love kisses
He'll make your face pay dear.

Sharing A Treat

Dividing something, half and half
doubles the sweetness of the treat,
cuts cost and calories in half,
and charms the moments spent, complete.

Sharing A Treat: Poems of Love and Friendship

A Day When Stones Cried Out Remembrance

"I tell you," [Jesus] replied, "if they keep quiet, the stones will cry out." (Luke 19:40)

Some things must be said, will be said. Silence is not an option. Some injustices must be named, will be named. Sacrifices deserve to be commemorated, insist on being commemorated. Good, and truth, and justice cannot go unnoted. If they are not given place history itself will rise up to give them a place. Pleasant times and unpleasant times equally deserve their say, each contributes to our store of knowledge from which we draw the materials to build the future.

It requires faith to believe James Russell Lowell's stirring words, "Truth forever on the scaffold, wrong forever on the throne, yet that scaffold sways the future, and behind the dim unknown, standeth God within the shadow, keeping watch above his own." But to choose not to believe them is to bear witness to the strength of wrong.

Honor the living, commemorate the dead, rejoice in tradition, usher in new ways, drive your vintage auto to the local car

A Day When Stones Cried Out: Remembrances

show, but take the newest model on your cross-country vacation.

A Day When Stones Cried Out: Remembrances

A Haiku For Lola

In Memory of Lola (Nichols) Swanson
(Jan. 10, 1931-Feb. 5, 2014)

*L*oving memories
*O*f one whose gentle *L*aughter
*A*lways brought us joy

Sunday Afternoons of Old

What were your Sunday afternoons like
In those day when you were young and free?
I'd love to know so I could enjoy them with you.
I'll tell you just a bit of mine and, if you wish,
You can share your times with me.

Summer Sundays were warm and steamy.
I have a harder time remembering
The wintry Sunday afternoons,
Though they must have been as
Numerous as were the steamy ones.

It was always good to get out of those
Fancy duds we wore to church.
I don't have a clear memory of the clothes
I got into – mostly hand-me-downs . . .
Not very exciting or memorable, I reckon.

A Day When Stones Cried Out: Remembrances

On ordinary days there would be a meal at home.
Sunday was a "meat" day, most likely chicken,
Or perhaps a meat-loaf or a pork roast.
Mashed potatoes, green beans, home-made bread
And peach cobbler are things remembered most.

If company came the meal changed little,
But the atmosphere a lot . . .
Uncles came – too late to go to church –
But never without opinions about God,
And church, and country.

There was never agreement on anything,
Or if there was it got lost under
An afternoon of heated debates;
"Comparisons of understandings."
I learned a lot I later had to "unlearn."

But uncles brought cousins, mostly male:
Some younger than me but mostly older,
And wiser in the ways of the world,
And willing – no, eager – to share their wisdom.
I learned a lot I later had to "unlearn."

Some Sundays were days for family
Drives into the countryside;
A time to see for the "thousandth" time –

A Day When Stones Cried Out: Remembrances

Though not without interest –
The places where "the folks" had lived.

Packing four – sometimes five – good-sized kids
Into the back seat of a Model-A Ford
Created an opportunity for many disputes,
Refereed by threats and "promises"
From the front, "promises" always fulfilled.

The fulfillment of "promises"
Was a regular part of Sunday activity.
Incidents invariably occurred at church,
Or on the way there, or back,
For which atonement had to be made.

Sunday afternoon was a time of rest –
Not inactivity – although that too, occasionally.
It was a time when "work" was laid aside
And games, and talk, and food, and family
Took their place at center stage.

Now we shape our Sundays differently.
Do we shape them well?
And could we, being who we are,
Shape them any differently
And still fulfill the things our hearts desire to do?

A Day When Stones Cried Out: Remembrances

An Old-Fashioned Christmas Card

Christmas cards – old-fashioned Christmas Cards,
Depicting snowy roads – high-banked snowy roads,
Are getting scarce – the paper kind we used to get are
Seldom sent these days – replaced by e-mail overload.

But God – the maker of all things, especially Christmas,
Has made, this year – at least up here where snow
Defines – is the essence of Wisconsin Christmas-card-ness,
A living – spell-bound, drive-through, Christmas show.

The streets, lawns, fields – the whole wide world is white;
Oaks, elms and ash – each lifts its snow-clad arms to heaven;
Pines – their branches laden with their diamond freight, fight
The wind – thieving wind, to keep the gift they're given.

And I, a child again – a simple snow adoring child again
Am awed that God – who has a thousand climes to deck,
Would stop – would lay aside His work, and go to pains
To paint a Christmas Card for me – and you as well, I reck.

A Day When Stones Cried Out: Remembrances

A Day When Stones Cry Out
(A Haiku Trio)

Ancient man piled rocks –
monuments of remembrance.
We should do no less.

Metaphorically
we raise edifices for
sacrifices past,

knowing that, though mute,
those "stones" will nonetheless cry
out that someone cared.

Arizona Tragedy
(A Haiku)

nineteen firemen died
to save the homes and lives of
those they hardly knew

A Day When Stones Cried Out: Remembrances

An *ism* With a Father's Heart

How do we define patriotism?
Is it defined by the amount of money given
by fat cats to support their favorite "ism,"
or by the years some poor doke rots in prison?

No, it is not a matter of the pocketbook,
not the domain of shades and crooks,
not the way one spins an issue's look,
not even ventures operated by the book.

Patriotism – take the word apart –
is an "ism" with a *father's* heart,
seeking all the good that it can start,
to benefit the *family* in all its varied parts.

The *family* in all its great variety;
all races, creeds, states, and ideologies,
living, working – co-existing – peacefully,
with the *pater's* benediction – patriotically.

When I Am Gone
The Art of Writing

How and where writing was born is a topic of great interest to students of human civilization. Perhaps first a tool of merchants, used to record their client's accounts, it soon became the near exclusive gift of scribes who used it to "inscribe" on stone and clay, and later on velum and papyrus, sacred texts that told the stories of their origins and recorded the holy laws that would guide the conduct of their societies.

The power of the scribe can be imagined in a time when even kings, many of whom were illiterate despite their immense power, depended upon them to translate the near magical symbols of the sacred texts or to convey in writing their decrees. To possess the ability to read and write was to assure oneself a position of honor and influence in an almost totally illiterate society.

There was a time when those who wished not to go on record avoided writing, preferring a face-to-face conversation because of its *deniability*. In our day of miniaturized digital video and audio equipment no one can be assured that their spoken words are not being recorded for future release. Prominent politicians – and unknown politicians, suddenly

When I am Gone: The Art of Writing

made prominent by revelations recorded and then released – provide recent proof that there are no safe secrets any longer.

But still many are reluctant to put their thoughts, beliefs, and especially their emotions "in print." Doing so subjects the author to all sorts of potential abuse and, perhaps more frightening, makes their words available for future generations to dissect, parse, and distort in ways unimaginable to their creator.

But thank God for those who have dared to write. They have enriched the world, quite literally in a few instances, figuratively in many more. At a time in human history when writing, for the masses, consists of brief tweets, or at most hastily and non-grammatically composed text messages crafted with abbreviations and emoticons, it is more essential than ever that we write – truly write – so that this gift from the dawn of civilization will not atrophy or die out in our day.

But what to write? Write poetry or prose. Write fact or fiction. Write technical manuals or popular "how to" books. Write about others (biography) or yourself (memoirs). Write poorly or well – let the future decide. But write. Leave it to fate, or the gods to decide what will remain and what will be valued. But write; it is our gift to the future, in a very real sense, the only way we can remain in this world after we are gone.

When I am Gone: The Art of Writing

Inbreathed
(A Haiku)

true inspiration
weaves words the author dare not
claim to be his own

Making Do With What I Have

One poet merely wishes to paint a picture,
not caring particularly whether any reader
sees in it the things he had in mind.

Another has a point to make; is stricter
in the choice she makes; as a pleader
for a cause her picture is a clearer kind.

Still another simply loves to work with words;
to weave a spell around a heart or shock
the reader into consciousness.

And then there's me – with one "vocal cord" –
ecstatic when words I write can half knock
out some accidental sagaciousness.

When I am Gone: The Art of Writing

A Two-line Poem

A one line poem is a practical impossibility,
But two can say, "I love you," perfectly!

When I Am Gone

Don't mess with my words!
I don't care what your motive is.

You may wish I had said something
    I purposely chose not to say,
or regret that I said something
    you wish I hadn't said.
You may be embarrassed
    at my uncouth words,
distressed at my punctuation,
tempted to enhance my legacy
    by "cleaning up" my work.

You may simply want to erase
    all memory of me.
(Good luck. That's been tried before.)

When I am Gone: The Art of Writing

If the Author of my words,
    the One in whom I live
    and breathe
    and have my being,
    deems my words worthy of
    continuation all you do
    will only cause them to
    live longer.

But just leave them lie, please.

I'll stand before the Great Judge
    and give account
    for every word ill-spoken –
    or well-written –
    even every thought.

I don't need you tampering with them
    in the interim.

So when I am gone,
    keep your hands off my words.
Let them speak to you
    from where they lie,
or not speak to you at all.

When I am Gone: The Art of Writing

Adjectives Are For Poets . . . Uh, Poor Poets

Authors writing papers with which to "snow"
a simple-minded reader;
news writers determined to make a show –
a "ratings" catcher,
are free to visit the website, "Adjectives to Go".
But any serious writer –
poets excepted – they're uniquely in the know –
prefers a solid "doer",
a truth-full *noun* or *verb* without a single bell or bow.

Wrecking Your Chances

Never write a poem when you are this tired;
it is bound to turn out badly, thus
wrecking any chance you could be hired
as the next laureate of the U.S.

The Value of a Dream
Poems About Fairie

Of all the histories left to us none exceed, in their power to move our hearts, those we label "myths." Someone once defined a myth as "that which never happened but is always true."

Curiously, the very oldest examples of non-commercial writing that have survived from the ancient world are mythical stories of the exploits of the gods, of human heroes, of cataclysmic events, of titanic movements of armies, of immense loves and hatreds shaping human history. These stories record, we presume, events that "never happened." But we continue to read and tell these tales – and even to weave new myths around them – because they are "always true;" they tell us the truth about human nature and the nature of the world in which humans live.

Children seem to live closest to Fairie – that land of myths which many adults have never entered or if they once did they have ceased to visit, having come to believe that such a land does not exist.

Still thousands of adults do enjoy visiting fantasy lands via gaming, videos (movies/TV), stage events, simulations, and

The Value of a Dream: Poems About Fairie

reading the works of great mythmakers. And children will never cease to find, on their own or in the company of a caring adult, the doorway into Fairie. Left to themselves they will invent whole worlds, peopled with creatures and events that "never existed" but with which they engage to help them make sense of the world in which they live day to day. And with the help of adults they can be led into more elaborate, and perhaps more truthful (more meaningful) worlds via the writing of great mythmakers, past and present.

Mankind will always live, one foot in Fairie and the other in what we call the real world. But we will never know for sure just where the boundary between the two worlds is drawn, if indeed there is a boundary between them.

The Value of a Dream: Poems About Fairie

Shadows

rushing westward,
streaming over undulating land,
ghosts of the morning
over-swarm the view;
climb the sides of hills,
leap tall buildings and run beyond,
always beyond,
racing to the far horizon;
fearing no terrain they
mark the hollows as though
to claim those spaces
as their rightful own;
strong redoubts against
the burning mid-day sun;

then, no sooner won,
their retreat's begun;
growing ever shorter hour by hour,
giving ground to coming day,
ceding territory quickly gained
in their hasty dash at dawn,
they lie deathly still at noon-tide,
mere pools of darkness
in a desert of burning light,
waiting for the signal to begin

The Value of a Dream: Poems About Fairie

their evening flight to darkness.

In their shadowless eastern home
they'll while the night,
hoping the next dawn will brightly
send them on their way again.

Legions of Darkness

Driving north in Minnesota
on Interstate Thirty-five
just before sunset,
I was startled to see,
a long line of shadows
silently rushing at me
from the west,
hugging the ground,
leaping over depressions,
flowing over obstacles
with an elasticity that science
has yet to master.

As they swept over the car
I recalled that my shadow –
an image of the van
that gave it birth –
had, just moments before,

The Value of a Dream: Poems About Fairie

been romping along
to the right of the car,
playfully shaping itself
to the contours of the land,
stretching farther
and farther afield
as the sun went down.

In panic I needed to
reign it in, to call it back,
but before I could speak
it had joined the dark legions
rushing away to the east,
driven by Sol's last beams,
and soon it was far beyond
the sound of my call.

At sunset the dark host,
its harvest of shadows in tow,
slipped over the eastern horizon,
beyond the pain of Sol's glance,
bearing my shadow away;
whether a prisoner of war
or a willing recruit
I will never know.

The Value of a Dream: Poems About Fairie

Firiel

Firiel!
Earth's daughter
(God's Child)
Destined to watch,
To wait, to while,
While loved ones sail
To shores you long to see.

Firiel!
Watch, wait,
And while beside the shore.
'Til, in God's good time
earth holds no more –
Then take my hand
And journey home with me.

The Value of a Dream: Poems About Fairie

Galadriel
(From her admirer, Gimli)

She comes in morning light
As though it were her right
To start the day for us.

She stands in rain or shine
Enclothed in robes as fine
As any other edifice,

And in her stately stance,
And in her humble glance,
Enfolds a world of care for us.

Her lovely, giving hands,
Are golden marriage bands
Bespeaking love continuous.

Her shining eyes reflect
The joy of her respect –
She sees the "gift of God" in us.

When evening shadows stretch,
Her love runs out to fetch
A *fairy* robe with which to cover us.

Galadriel, Queen of all our hearts,
Who else but she could play the part –
Our heart's beloved philanthropist.

The Value of a Dream: Poems About Fairie

Morning in a Fairie Glen

I awakened in a fairie glen,
With dancing elves who vanished when
I tried to cast my eyes on them.
But one I saw who did not disappear,
But rather came to me and showed no fear;
A fairie Queen I saw – up close and clear.

The Value of a Dream

Dreams are timeless spaces –
Elven-fashioned places –
Where hearts, with interlocking paces,
Stroll a path that endlessly retraces
Hopes that earth-time fain effaces.

To Fairie and Back on a Foggy Morning

In the cool heavy morning air,
things once clearly seen are
shadows only of their former selves;
I move as though among the elves.

The Value of a Dream: Poems About Fairie

The world, reduced to half a block
draws all waters through its lock,
drowning views once far away
that I observed on clearer days.

This misty day I am content
to chance with wraiths of veiled intent;
and concentrate my straining gaze
on things with which they would amaze.

———

Ground spiders' well-wrought
snares, unseen in ordinary airs,
lie waiting, visible in scores
upon the lawns, their open doors
collecting dew – for what?
To quaff some insect's thirst
and make it spider's prey
to satisfy a lust for blood?

———

My friend, the "three-wheel biker,"
materializes slowly from the fog –
walking still – some teen-age thieves
robbed him of his wheels.

The Value of a Dream: Poems About Fairie

I approach, "Have you heard anything
about your bike?"

He stops and turns his headphones off.
"No, I'll probably never see the
G_ _ D_ _ _ _ _ thing again."

He showed some pieces
they'd strewn along their path.
"They must have stole the
G_ _ D_ _ _ _ _ thing just
for the Hell of tearing it up."

His face lights up, "But my renter's
insurance is paying for most of it."

He darkens once again, "I suppose they'll
want the money back if it is found."

My assurance to the contrary
seems to bring some comfort.

"I've got a new one ordered
from the cities." He smiles.

I lay a hand on his shoulder
and tell him I'm so glad for him . . .

The Value of a Dream: Poems About Fairie

"I've thought about you
so many times since yesterday."

He turns his headphones up;
we fade, back to back,
each from each,
dissolving slowly into fog,
neither knowing either's name.

The albino squirrel may be
scampering up the oaks
in the big yard with the
"For Sale" sign in it,
but the fog is too heavy to tell.
Each tree assumes an elven shape
in the misty morning light.
I wonder if the squirrel knows
the value of his real estate.

The new bypass has jumbled
all the streets and changed their names;
I'm never really sure just where it is I'm at.
This morning, in the fog, it's almost matterless;
mere shapes and sounds, the scent of
dew-heavy grasses penetrate

The Value of a Dream: Poems About Fairie

the senses close at hand.
It is a *perfect* place to be.

———————

Finding my way under the highway,
up the newly named "Pine Lodge Road,"
to the north entrance to the cemetery,
I enter, where I've lately chosen to walk.

The cemetery, longer north to south
than east to west, has a paved road
girding its perimeter, with another
cutting the oval in two
from north to south,
and yet another from west to east,
forming a cross I suppose,
unless it was made for children
playing Fox and Geese.
There is a shrine where
the crossing roads intersect.
It is a Catholic Cemetery.

I walk the perimeter,
starting on the eastern side.
The lawn, heavy with dew is filled
with ominous ground spider traps.

The Value of a Dream: Poems About Fairie

Trees hang low over the road
waiting to drench me if I dare
to brush against them.

Turning on the south end,
heading west, I see a bunny,
trapped along the chain-link fence.
She/he waits to see
if I will really pass that way,
relaxed but watchful,
growing more concerned,
and then alarmed as I draw close.
I try to pass in such a way
that my passing will not alarm . . .
she/he stiffens, makes a couple
of futile attempts to find a hole
in the fence, and then resigns
herself/himself to whatever
fate I decree. I can feel
its pulse decrease as I walk on.

On the south to north, west-side drive
the trees are nearly all apple,
mostly ornamental crabs,
but one appears to be an
"ordinary" crab.

The Value of a Dream: Poems About Fairie

They are filled with fruit,
"pregnant" is the only word
to describe the swelling green
of the "ordinary" tree.
I'll try to be there when she
"delivers" in the fall.
Thievery? No midwifery!

Turning east again on the
north-end road a man
emerges from the fog.
Both startled, we say,
"Hello," and I exclaim
what a beautiful day it is.
I wished, almost as soon
as he had disappeared
into the fog, that I had said,
"What a day, God has given us!"
A Catholic sexton
would appreciate that.
So slow of thought!
Forgive me Lord.

———————

Leaving the cemetery I return
to what may be the intersection
of Pine Lodge Road and East Hamilton

The Value of a Dream: Poems About Fairie

and take what could be Hamilton
north past Robin School.
The school is only a dark square
to the right; to the left, a
newly formed bank of the
freeway bypass lies neatly curbed
and sown with clovers,
wild-flowers, and grasses.

Further north, adjacent to the
barely visible Harvestime Church,
the new curb is already completely
overhung with the gold of
bird-foot trefold.
(Is that what we learned to call it?)

The street back to Pine Lodge Road
leads through a new development
with quaffed lawns, symmetrically
planted boulevards, and lawn sprinkling
systems, busy with their morning chores,
oblivious to the fact that their host-lawns
have no need of watering this morning.

The Value of a Dream: Poems About Fairie

The safety of the neighborhood
is heralded by garage doors
left open through the night.
My mind turns to benighted places
where all the locks in all the world
could not guarantee this tranquility.

Thanking God, not without a sense
of guilt, for the blessings I enjoy,
I hurry on to Pine Lodge Road.

———————

My 2.8 mile walk takes me
fifty minutes or so to complete
but I'm making good time today.
Passing again under the freeway
I'm aware that the sun is trying
to lift the fog. Cars a block away
might be distinguished by their
makes if one had eyes capable
of making out their makes
in a fog like this.
The ground-spider webs,
if they are meant for traps,
have failed their maker's aims;
I've yet to see a spider at its work
nor anything caught in its web.

The Value of a Dream: Poems About Fairie

With relief I conclude that the webs
must serve only to collect water.
Clearly I've misjudged spiders
all these years.

Passing the point where my biker friend
and I had exchanged greetings
I say a thanks for his good fortune.

Alas, the sun seems, after all,
to be losing the battle.
As I arrive home the sky
is heavy and grey again.
I'm warm from walking.
My clothes hang damp from fog.
But I've seen things, close up, that
might have been missed on other days:

- spider webs,
- an old friend,
- elven shapes,
- a frightened hare,
- pregnant trees,
- coexisting plants,
- a sleepy neighborhood,
- the sun struggling to reclaim its world.

The Value of a Dream: Poems About Fairie

Back at my computer,
ready to do some work,
and *look* . . .
on the hair of my arms . . .
a hundred sparkling diamonds!

*I've been to Fairie and back,
and I am richer for the journey.*

Sun-Dappled Days

It's been a golden-dappled day
in which I've walked a shaded way,
watching shadow elves display
their dancing form – a wild foray;
from golden ray to golden ray
they danced and whiled the day away.

Tomorrow, if I have my say,
I'll keep the clouds at bay,
granting me one more display
of wily light wraiths at their play,
running on the path ahead to lay
a thoroughfare of golden leis.

Spider Lives
Prophetic Poems

Prophets are a misunderstood lot. Consequently many of them have died at the hands of those who misunderstood them; even more at the hands of those who understood them all too well.

I grew up among prophets, many of whom did not understand their true purpose. Thinking themselves bound to foretell the future they often made fools of themselves and brought discredit to the God for whom they professed to speak.

A prophet is one who sees an evil and speaks against it. Our best view of prophets comes from the pages of Holy Scripture. Indeed there were times when those prophets foretold events that were to come but most of the time they simply spoke as emissaries of God, calling the society back into the paths of righteousness from which it so easily strayed.

It was assumed that the prophet was moved by, and spoke under the inspiration of the Spirit of God. There were true prophets, false prophets, prophets for hire, and prophets who could not be bought.

All nations – all cultures – have their prophets. Rarely are they honored. Only a handful of their contemporaries typically

Spider Lives: Prophetic Poems

recognize them as the voice of one crying in the wilderness, "Make a straight path for God." The urge is to give them as wide a berth as possible. They sound like cranks and often look a little seedy. (The prophet business doesn't usually pay enough to afford Hart Schaffner Marx labels.) In fact a prophet, too well fed, and too fashionably clad, is very likely not "the voice of God."

But it is dangerous to dismiss a prophet too cavalierly. God clothes his messengers in all manner of garb. It is the message that needs to be examined more than the messenger. And poor indeed is any society that has no true prophets.

Spider Lives: Prophetic Poems

Watching An Old Man Outlive His Wisdom

I've watched an old man become a fool,
throw away a trove of Godly wisdom;
become the willing but unwitting tool
of those who, caring not a whit for the halidom
he had constructed to the glory of God's rule,
cared only to advance *their* earthly kingdom.

This poor modern Hezekiah should have died
two decades sooner, before his judgment failed.
In youth, like his sad ancient counterpart, he had cried
against idolatry, but in old age, pride prevailed –
inviting Babylon's emissaries in, he crucified
the Son afresh and, at Babylon's golden altars, dallied.

The Prophet in the Wilderness – Marilynne Robinson

Meanwhile, the messenger who had gone off to summon Micaiah advised him, "Look, everything that the other prophets were saying was unanimously favorable to the king. So please, cooperate with them and speak favorably."
                    (1Ki 22:13 International Standard Version)

So should the prophet speak according to her lights
or according to the "lights" of those,
who, fearing controversy – to avoid a fight –
silence those who know, and know they know?

Spider Lives: Prophetic Poems

Micaiah spent some time on stale bread and water
for sharing with king Ahab his lights.
Though coached in advance – told the words he should utter –
he laid out the hard truth in plain sight.

All should read a book by Marilynne Robinson'
The Death of Adam; a strong critique
of Darwinian thought, [1] a prophet's orison,
a prayer that Adam will come awake,

shake off the spell that Darwinian prophets cast,
a God defying, God denying,
death-dealing doctrine of survival of the best
which rapes the earth and leaves it dying.

With poetic power the prophet loudly cries.
Four hundred hundred, her words defy,
who dance and pipe the "established truth", Satan's lie:
"Eat this fruit; it will not make you die."

---

[1] *Robinson does not deny scientific evolution, nor does she subscribe to a young earth theory. But she sees as pernicious – even fatal to the human race – the social, political, and environmental uses of the doctrine of survival of the fittest.*

Spider Lives: Prophetic Poems

Weekend Fare

It is Friday afternoon;
We've watched the early evening news.
It always seems as soon
as news is done the networks choose
to play a weekend "tune"
in which the looming crises lose
their urgency; a boon,
I guess, to marketers of booze,
and sports and Looney Tunes.

**A Long Journey Back to Where We Began:
Hanging our Thoughts on a Vapor**

There was a day when man's thoughts,
sub-lim or self-consciously fraught,
were kept secure for his time;
kept safe in the vault of his mind.

But thoughts kept in a mind –
a mere vapor adrift in time –
are lost when the mind wafts away
or rots under six feet of clay.

And, alas, thoughts transmitted by
words are prone too to die;

Spider Lives: Prophetic Poems

drifting and shifting they wend
their way in an unsteady wind.

Ancients attempted to store thoughts away;
to make them forever endure,
engraved on stone, solid and sure,
or baked hard on tablets of clay.

Parchment, pottery; each gave way,
to paper, walls of deep canyons and caves,
bones, seashells, the handles of staves –
as man preserved his musings and raves.

'Til they crumbled or rotted away,
leaving those holding the fragments
the task of discerning, among the rents,
meanings lost in the frequent lacunae.

Ashurbanipal's "books", locked away
in archives, guarded by scribes and slaves,
only by accident survived 'til the day
they would be known – for a while – by posterity.

Compiled in books and stored in archives,
the wisdom of man has fought to survive
despite the ravage of war, weather, and time,
to say nothing of the censor's arrogant pride.

Spider Lives: Prophetic Poems

Now we've begun to presumptuously store
our thoughts in an ephemeral "Cloud" –
without weight or substance, our digital lore
resides at the will of the Keepers of Clouds.

So we're back again to no guarantee –
mischief or "outage" may conspire to betray
the hope for which we trustingly pay;
In one instant, the Clouds may be swept away.

**Justice, Blind Justice
(A Haiku Quartet)**

If George is pronounced
blameless then Trayvon had no
right to "stand *his* ground"

Trayvon is beyond
questioning and George is judged
innocent – case closed

The wanabee cop
can return to the beat, an
NRA hero

Spider Lives: Prophetic Poems

Fathers, keep your sons
at home at night; the night is
full of wanabees

The Human Malady

Desiring what isn't paid for
may be the second "root of all evil";
"love of money" being nothing more
than a new name for "civil".

Begging for a handout isn't just a fault
of those with nothing they can pay;
as often, those with bulging vaults
are raking unearned pelf their way.

The over-charging lawyer, the underpaying pimp
really play the same game;
The million dollar "ministry", the town skimp –
Just twins, with a different name.

A tax exemption or a disability allotment –
each a good (or bad) public policy –
is nonetheless an unpaid "got-ment",
compliments of a taxpaying citizenry.

Spider Lives: Prophetic Poems

The rich begrudge a bowl of porridge,
the poor resent a life of ease,
unwilling, each, to bridge
the gulf of mutual oblige.

**Standing Watch: Questions for
an Ancient Tree in a Chicago Park**

Yellow tape defines a space;
anchored to a pole that holds,
suspended overhead,
a backboard and a hoop;
wrapped around a tree
whose ancient girth
seems capable of
enfolding eight of the slender,

Spider Lives: Prophetic Poems

blue-clad men standing watch
over the bloody scene of
thirteen attempted murders;
young men they –
trained and badged to watch –
born more than a century
after the wizened tree
began its watch over . . .
who remembers what;
a farm yard, a city lawn,
and now at last, a battlefield,
parading as a children's
playground?

Does it grieve –
this perennial giant –
remembering other days
when carefree hearts
enjoyed its shade,
raced to climb its heights,
freely shared its joys,
or does it merely
bear mute witness to
a city's daily slaughter;
just so much more
of what its leaves have
had to cover – every fall –

a century's worth of falling;
watching reds, yellows,
browns – the precious gold
of every Autumn –
covered with the pallid,
white of every Winter,
rising in virulent passion
every new Summer?

Mikhail Kalashnikov, How Do I Love Thee?

Love is measured by constancy,
excusing a multitude of sins,
finding reasons to insistently
forgive the sinner time and time again.

The trail of betrayals is never so long –
we've lost sight of its beginning –
that it stills the fawning suitor's song.
So the lover, unfettered, goes on sinning.

In Tucson, Virginia Tech, Aurora, Columbine,
Chicago, Sandy Hook, Ft. Hood, D.C.,
Oak Creek; a persistent, bloody line
stretches on as far as human eye can see.

Spider Lives: Prophetic Poems

And still the frightened lift their lover's song,
still, and still again, forgive their lover's sins,
quick to blame their lover's many wrongs
on any cause, or anyone, or anything but him.

How do I love thee, Kalashnikov? Let me count.
Can hate, or wounds, or weekly mayhem,
pooling blood, shattered lives, or any amount
of heinous sins you've sinned, my ardor stem?

No. None! It is a lover's rights that are at stake.
When public parks, shopping malls, and gated lawns
are changed to killing fields, your thirst you slake
with brother-blood: an AK-47 thrills until the ammo's gone.

Spider Lives: Prophetic Poems

Grieving the Uses of BG

BG has spoken – spoken well – spoken truth.
His cords once strong and filled with youth –
ringing unafraid, undefiled, and couth –
now frail with age can barely move.

But electronics serve to prop an old man up,
keep him speaking long beyond his years;
speaking long since his words, now served up
in fragments, brought spirit-meaning to our ears.

BG no longer hears the prophet call anew,
but *those who need his name* are not averse
to sustaining the ruse, whatever they must do;
ghost write a book, create a film, or worse

insinuate their will and plans into his will,
speak "in his name" and make the claim,
though voice and body fails, he's speaking still.
But not, alas, with prophet voice of BG fame.

Oh lord, preserve your servant's legacy;
preserve the decades spent in service *willingly*,
against the thieves who, working stealthily,
weave only badly muddled memories.

Spider Lives: Prophetic Poems

Believe Me, We Are Awash in Anonymity

". . . a *senior* counterterrorism official, who, like half a dozen other *top* intelligence, law enforcement and diplomatic officials interviewed for this article, spoke on the condition of anonymity because he did not want to be identified discussing delicate national security issues." (Bolding was in the original article)

(From *Syria Militants Said to Recruit Visiting Americans to Attack U.S.*, New York Times, Jan. 9, 2013, Michael S. Schmidt and Eric Schmidt. Subsequently quoted in more than a dozen other online commentaries.)

Seven Haiku For Anonymity

Anonymity
is the refuge of cowards,
puffers, and scammers.

Anonymity
in a coward's hand is a
back ally mugging

Anonymity
in the hand of a puffer
is a poised dagger

Spider Lives: Prophetic Poems

Anonymity
in the hand of a scammer
steals a poor man's wealth

Anonymity
in the hand of the righteous
is a sacred trust

Anonymity
in the cause of good corrupts
the good cause it serves

Transparency *is*
truth: anonymity is
a veil, shielding lies

The Righting of the Costa Concordia

The "gleaming beauty" is aright again
slowly plying for the scrap heap
her rusting form justly linked in sin
with her faithless Captain's creep
to safety masquerading in
a woman's dress as women leapt
to certain death who could not swim.

Spider Lives: Prophetic Poems

Perverting a Good Thing
(*However, the wisdom that comes from above is first of all pure, then peace-loving, gentle, willing to yield, full of compassion and good deeds and without a trace of partiality or hypocrisy.*)
Jas. 3:17

People who speak self-servingly –
    Performers speaking obscenely,
    Poets speaking obliquely,
    Politicians speaking misleadingly,
    Power speaking arrogantly,
    Pornographers speaking indecently,
    Panderers speaking beguilingly,
    Professors speaking haughtily,
    Preachers speaking timidly,
    Provocateurs speaking irresponsibly,
    Purveyors speaking deceptively,
    Profiteers speaking clandestinely,
    Prognosticators speaking unremittingly,
    Patricians speaking condescendingly,
    Peasants speaking envyingly –
Pervert the potential of speech.

Spider Lives: Prophetic Poems

Bucking the Lord's Day

Pews ordinarily full
have scattered empty spaces,
showing the Lord lacks the pull
of bucks at fifty paces.

Against Blind Intolerance of Islam

"...let the one who has never sinned
throw the first stone!" John 8:7 (NLT)

The only religion Jesus criticized
was the one he honored
by his faithful attendance
at the synagogue.

So why have you, his followers, politicized,
yes, with Satan, cosponsored
a relentless campaign of discordance,
against another's god?

Is there not plank enough in your eyes –
sin enough in you to be deplored –
without proclaiming your intolerance
of another's god?

Spider Lives: Prophetic Poems

Was it hateful diatribes that seized
your heart and mind, or
love and grace, a preponderance
of the love of God?

You are not called to demonize,
but to evangelize, to open doors,
to show through your long sufferance
the saving love of God.

Your "enemy" is not to be despised,
demonized, ridiculed or
destroyed, but – surprise – *romanced*
into the kingdom of God.

**Aerial Warfare
(A Haiku Trio)**

High, high, high atop
the pine a winged one, silent,
silent, scans the scene.

Far, far, far below
the pine tree counsels footed
ones, "Hide here. Hide there."

Spider Lives: Prophetic Poems

No friend to winged ones,
he. "Be gone," he cries, "Be gone!"
"Spare the footed ones."

Spider Lives

A tiny little spider life
summarily smudged out
leaving an almost imperceptible
smear on the computer screen
inspired contemplation of
a spider's place
in the scheme of creation.

Ten thousand spiders crowd a square
and in their pride make claim
to be significant,
demanding that another spider
whom they hate
be smudged out so that yet
another can be given place.

Two spiders meet
in a gated town
on a dark and rainy street
each supposing each to be his enemy
each "stands his ground"

Spider Lives: Prophetic Poems

the spider with the stronger
venom wins, smudging out his foe.

Three hundred spiders
crowded in a steel cocoon
drift across an ocean
to crash to earth
sparing some
maiming some
smudging out the unlucky few.

Oh You who sees the sparrow fall,
who grows the lily tall,
who counts the hairs on
balding heads,
show us You're aware
and that You care
that tiny spiders die.

Do you not know that I
who spun the web of galaxies
came to your spiders' world
in spider form
and faced the rage
of spider hate
to save your spider race?

Spider Lives: Prophetic Poems

Don't Forget To Send In The Cash

The TV preacher offers to pray for your needs,
and requests thirty dollars to serve as a "seed".

The Party's "quick survey," seeking your thoughts,
includes a reminder to send your "hard fought."

The Doctors – especially Oz – to "help you stay well,"
bring on slick hucksters with something to sell.

CVS, in a fit of "conscience" has ceased to sell smokes,
but candy, soda, quack cures, they'll sell to poor folks.

"Buyer beware" is the buyer's defense;
standing alone – and standing against.

And They Say The Taxes Are Eating Us Alive!

I just finish roughing out
my 2013 federal taxes.
For my wife and I, about –
after Turbo Tax axes,
through credits and deductions,
an impressive chunk of change –
the cost, upon careful calculation,
of a cup each of Caribou per day.
Where, such a bargain,
but in the U.S.A.?

Spider Lives: Prophetic Poems

Praying for Nero
(1Timothy 2:1,2)

That we may live quiet and peaceful lives.
To that end, we are admonished to pray
for those whose actions drive
us to distraction; those whose ways,

we fear, will sweep away the good
that good men labored long
to fashion; truths that stood
against the "lying throng".

That our lives may be pacific;
that our hearts may be at peace;
we pray a prayer specific
for the "foeman" we perceive,

and in praying thus, we still
our troubled hearts – and a
faith-full heart thus stilled, will
perceive its "enemy" another way.

Spider Lives: Prophetic Poems

**Hand-me-down Warfare –
A Meditation from a Lover of Fireworks**

Have you wondered if our fascination with –
to say nothing of our participation in –
sport, is vicarious; a venting of our ancient faith
that winners are righteous, losers have sinned?

What shame it is to win the penultimate round,
then not succeed in clinching the final crown.
"Clinch the crown!" – a linguistic clue, full-blown,
that sport is warfare's hand-me-down.

And every 4th of July the rockets' red glare –
the thud of bombs bursting in air –
allow us to stand in safety and stare;
enjoying a "battle" without being *there*.

The day will include a *contest* or two –
all cheer for the hometown boys to triumph.
The feasting, and drinking, and hullabaloo,
ends in a flash, flare, and chest-filling thump.

The swoosh, the fire, and the thunder
stir ancient tribal instincts that we
cannot indulge and not wonder
how truly devoted to peace we may be.

Spider Lives: Prophetic Poems

The Cost of a Burger
Just Thinkin' Out Loud

When I ask my friend a question that I thought his expertise should allow him to answer definitively, he merely said to me, "Think about it."

I thought about it and concluded that he didn't know the answer either and so invited me to solve the problem using pure reasoning. I've been thinking about it for forty years and still have no answer. Someday I'll Google it and then I'll have an answer.

In the case of practical problems, such as that which I proposed to my friend, we want definitive answers, answers that will stand the test of time and will not deceive us in a moment of need. But there are "problems" for which no definitive answers have been found, indeed may never be found. Are we to simply not think about them? Can we not think about them? Many of them impinge upon our deepest feelings, relate to our deepest needs. We *must* think about them, and we do.

Roughly speaking, that kind of thinking is called *philosophy*, a combination of ancient Greek words which mean love of

The Cost of a Burger: Just Thinkin' Out Loud

wisdom. When we ask, "Why did Mary die so young?" and try to solve the riddle of premature death we are engaging in philosophy. When we ask why humans avoid pain and seek pleasure we are, again, practicing philosophers.

Formal (professional) philosophers have special rules by which they gauge their logic and judge the soundness of their conclusions, but those of us who practice the art in its lesser forms are content to test our conclusions against our day to day experience. We are "common sense" philosophers. And as long as we are not selling our expertise to anyone that is probably good enough.

The following poems are the work of an arm-chair philosopher. If they trigger some thoughts for you they've done their work. Consider putting down your thoughts for those who follow you. Then leave them in some public place where they can be found.

The Cost of a Burger: Just Thinkin' Out Loud

Thank God For Words

Words are so inadequate to tell
the thoughts and feelings;
the love that swells our hearts.

But think, my friends,
if we had feelings –
joys and hopes without an end –
but words had not been formed,
their bliss to tell.

Thank God for words –
poor, clumsy, fumbling tools –
an equal gift to sages and to fools.

Thank God, with words
He made a wondrous way,
His love for us –
and ours for Him –
to say.

Let's "borrow" them
to use as friend-love's tools.

The Cost of a Burger: Just Thinkin' Out Loud

Should I Join Facebook?
(A reply to an e-mail query)

As a "nearly 80" sort of guy
I'm not up on all the latest fads,
but still, I find a lot of reasons why
I shouldn't tag them all as bad.

Because . . .

The spell-checking word processor's
saved my butt a million times
with its squiggly red reminders
filling nearly every line.

And when I'm stuck in no-no land
with a car that doesn't want to run
it's nice to have a phone at hand
to save me walking in the cold or sun.

And that GPS is the slickest thing around;
it can navigate at night or under rainy skies,
in heavy traffic and in unknown towns,
reading signs too faded for my failing eyes.

The best of all the gadgets that I've got
Is the "Streamer" that connects my cell-phone

The Cost of a Burger: Just Thinkin' Out Loud

to my hearing aids, though I admit I've got
some wondering if I'm talking to my clone.

However . . .

Facebook doesn't appeal to me;
nor does Skype – I've tried the latter.
It has nothing to do with technology;
it's my "face" that makes me shudder.

Still . . .

When I think of all the sweat and inefficiency
of my father's day, or even mine,
I thank the Lord for every modern ingenuity
that eases pain or saves some time.

The Hurt and the Hurter
(A Haiku Meditation)

If love never hurts
It isn't love after all –
Hurt attests to love

To love is to hurt
Only lovers can be hurt –
God hurts those he loves

The Cost of a Burger: Just Thinkin' Out Loud

God loves those he hurts
He hurt the one he loved most –
Love hurts the hurter

The hurt and hurter
Through hurt are drawn together –
Love never ceases

Hurt will pass away
Love sends it to extinction
Love lasts forever

Let There Be Light
(A Haiku Quartet)

While growing old, Lord,
I need especially to
see the brighter side

Eyes grown dim are prone
to see all things in shades of
gray, or worse, in black

Foresee my need; shine
a brighter light on things my

The Cost of a Burger: Just Thinkin' Out Loud

dull perception hides

Let there be light – sun
by day and moon by night – to
compensate my lack.

What Is The Cost of a Burger?

Mr. Bitman of the NYT
and his intern David Prentice
are trying to make us see
the cost of burger in practice.

"Price is not cost," says Bitman,
as any sensible eater can see.
Price, is a mere trifle, a sham;
is to cost as puddle to sea.

Price is the cost that the eater,
thoughtlessly gnawing his fare,
imagines equal to the burger
consumed without fanfare or flair.

But to know the true cost of a thing
one need only consider what's lost;
in the case of the burger what's missing
is the *life* of the bull who bore the *cost*.

The Cost of a Burger: Just Thinkin' Out Loud

Who Is My Friend

He was my neighbor,
Though I was not his neighbor;
I . . . invisible.

I was her neighbor,
Though she was not my neighbor;
She . . . beyond the pale.

Who is my neighbor;
Who names me as her friend or
Whom I name my friend?

Things Missed and Things Missed

Some things are missed
 a fault of
 auditory failure
Some things are missed
 because their
 essence always lingers

The preacher's softly
 urgent words

The Cost of a Burger: Just Thinkin' Out Loud

    of admonition
A child's babbled
    silly-serious
    inarticulation

The comic's denouement
    a quick and muted
    twist of wit
A shower's rapprochement
    with a roof
    that's loving it

The weather person's
    hurried need
    to say it all
A wind gust driven
    turgid against
    the north side wall

The grind of traffic's
    engines in the
    street below
A blind benefic
    rumble with a
    storm in tow

The Cost of a Burger: Just Thinkin' Out Loud

The breathy secret
    that implies the
    meeting is ad hoc
A consistent fret
    of ticking by the
    ancient windup clock

Some things are missed
    a fault of
    auditory failure
Some things are missed
    because their
    essence always lingers

The High Price of Aging
  (A Haiku Lament)

Care-free years of rest:
the cost-free port young and old
point their craft toward

Alas, the winds of
fate conspire; set a course not
wholly theirs to chose

The Cost of a Burger: Just Thinkin' Out Loud

Pain: the price they're asked
to pay for a berth in the
harbor called "Old Age"

Still few captains turn
their ships away from any
haven holding life

Our Final Resting Place
(Haiku Musings)

Moving on, seeking
our final resting place – we're
partial to *East Ridge*.

I know, I know, it
sounds like a cemetery –
you know, like *East Lawn*.

Tired of ownership
we're moving on with lighter
step, or will be soon.

Right now we're sorting,
packing for a move, a sale,
and give-a-ways too.

The Cost of a Burger: Just Thinkin' Out Loud

We end each day with
heavy steps and aching bones,
taking strength, on loan

from younger men, who
bound where we can merely creep,
lift what age cannot.

We'll get to *East Ridge,*
our final resting place here
on this weary earth,

And as for *East Lawn,*
we'll skip it all together –
ashes to ashes, we.

Shredding (1952 – 2014)

I've been shredding the past,
tax returns from 'fifty-two,
letters to and from a cast
of characters I knew
in days now dim with age,
receipts and cancelled checks,
attempts to play the sage.

The Cost of a Burger: Just Thinkin' Out Loud

Yellowed pages bow their necks
to the modern guillotine,
filling bag after bulging bag,
soon to be bleached clean,
recycled into pulpy slag.

I've been shredding decades of blessings,
memories sweet, and bitter sorrows;
shredding to avert the guessings
of some guessers some tomorrow.

The Cost of a Burger: Just Thinkin' Out Loud

A Borning Light
Poems of Faith

As I write this I'm reflecting on the fact – I believe it is a fact – that much of our media and popular culture is devoted to destroying our faith. Not just our faith in God, although that is the most pernicious manifestation of the fact. But for a long time now there has been a concerted, if not always conscious, campaign to debunk ideas and institutions that have been the pillars of our culture.

Beginning in the late 1970s politicians found that they could get laughs, and more importantly votes, with lines like, "Hello, I'm from the government and I'm here to help you." The clear implication being that the government *never* is there to help but rather to restrict freedom. Now, as this is being written in the fall of 2014, the crop of cynicism sown by those politicians has matured and we are struggling to know how to avoid having to harvest it and eat it.

Our artists, authors, and producers of media have fed us, for several decades, a diet of narcissism mixed with negativism, a deadly potion that destroys our ability to trust anyone; the police, our teachers, ministers, doctors, lawyers, to name only a few. Unfaithfulness in marriage, politics, religion, friendships are passed over as though of little consequence. Yesterday's lawbreaker is tomorrow's commentator on

A Borning Light: Poems of Faith

FoxNews or MSNBC. Garbage parades as truth across the Internet. E-mails forwarded by "Christian believers" are as filled with lies as anything in the secular media.

Is it any wonder that Jesus asked his disciples the question, *"When the son of man comes, will he find faith on the earth."*

I want to believe that he will. But Jesus' words are a challenge to those who cherish truth, and *faithfulness*. Faith will not survive without the active faithfulness of those who are devoted to it. It is not a perennial. It must be planted year after year, cultivated, propagated, guarded. It must be born witness to even in hostile environments. It may someday, and in some places, require the blood of martyrs to sustain it.

Is it worth such strenuous and dangerous exertion? The answer to that question is supplied by another question, "What will the world be like when/if faith is totally extinguished from our culture or our world?"

Jesus also said to his disciples, *"You are the salt of the earth . . . you are the light of the world."* God forbid that the salt would, in our day, lose its saltiness, that the light would be hidden under a bushel.

I intend all my poetry – and all my life – to reflect my faith, but the poems that follow I have judged to be more explicitly about faith and thus offer them under that heading.

A Borning Light: Poems of Faith

Treasures in Earthen Vessels

Ἔχομεν δὲ τὸν θησαυρὸν τοῦτον
ἐν ὀστρακίνοις σκεύεσιν
*We have this treasure in earthen
vessels 2 Cor. 4:7*

Humble terra cotta pots measure
out the potter's window shelf
each treasure treasured for the treasure
held, each treasured in itself.

The Serpent In Eden
(A Haiku Quartet)

He lives in Eden.
At no time, at no place, has
adam had so much.

*H*e finds no joy there.
The Serpent won't let *him* be
content in Eden.

He only values
Eden looking back, through a
gate of no return.

A Borning Light: Poems of Faith

Adam, forever
scorning Eden, forever
losing paradise.

This Day
(A Haiku)

This day I rise, a
grace-saved sinner – may this day
be a grace-shared day

A Haiku for Sinners

Caught in the act, bare-
naked – clothed again in Grace
that says, "Sin no more."

Your Presence
(A Haiku Trio)

To sense Your presence
Is my spirit's great desire;
Lay Your hand on me.

If rebuke alone
Brings your hand to rest on me
Then, Lord, let it be.

A Borning Light: Poems of Faith

A rebuke, indeed,
Coming from Your hand, tells me
That you care for me.

Four (or Five) Haiku Proverbs

Wisdom outweighs "smarts"
Taken apart, wisdom is
gold, "smarts" . . . rusting tin

Wisdom, eternal,
witnesses the parade of
"facts" quickly fading

Time, judge of all things –
callous revealer – peels off
the rotting veneer

Today's swagger is
tomorrow's embarrassment,
tomorrow's disgrace

Wisdom outweighs "smarts"
Taken – apart – wisdom is
gold, "smarts" . . . rusting tin

A Borning Light: Poems of Faith

An Easter Haiku

Our Lord is risen
Against all hope He conquered
death so we could live

A Borning Light

A spark
was all I saw at first –
a little burst of sunshine
beaming out amidst
a mist of flaxen hair –
backlit by window light.

Inspired
by a friend she spied –
ten years her senior,
whose turn to see her
thrilled her infant heart –
she flashed a golden smile.

The gathered,
solemn, come to grieve –
a sun long bright
now shone no more,
except in memory –
are lit by borning light.

A Borning Light: Poems of Faith

Simple Faith
(A Haiku)

They chide simple faith
but faith that isn't simple
isn't faith at all.

A (Haiku) Gospel Quartet

The Son is saying
"Come, trust in me, and be
reconciled to God."

For God so loved the
world that he gave his only
Son to die for it.

The Son came not to
condemn the world but that through
Him it could be saved.

All who call on His
name, and put their trust in Him,
have eternal life.

A Borning Light: Poems of Faith

résumé

no connection to
the mighty,
the well known,
the respected,
the wealthy

only twice perhaps
in the home
of a leader
and then to be
scrutinized, criticized

hung out with
tax collectors,
law breakers,
prostitutes,
and malefactors

born,
raised,
lived,
died,
indigent

seeks position
on earth –
as in heaven –
as King of Kings;
Lord of Lords

A Borning Light: Poems of Faith

Fall Colors Make Me Believe

There is a reason for everything,
I'm convinced of it;
whether the hand of God *shaped* each thing,
or He fashioned it
in a *thought-full* manner of making –
like, *Big Banging* it –
doesn't change the Genesis saying;
for me, confirms it;
"In the beginning *God* was making;"
I just believe it.

An Old Man's Dilemma
(A Haiku)
Philippians 1:21

The old man wobbled
between two options; live now
or live forever.

A Borning Light: Poems of Faith

He Comes
(A Haiku Quartet)

He will not consent
to be *crammed* into any
hostile place – He *comes*

When the darkness "ruled"
the deep, His Spirit *came* and
hovered over it

Earth shook its iron-mailed
fist at Him and still He *came*,
a helpless infant.

He *came* to His own
and they would not receive him.
but to those who would . . .

No Shame In Going Home

There is no shame in going home,
no shame in saying, "It was wrong to leave,"
no disgrace, leaving what was wrong
to bow to Truth, confessing, "Now I see."

A Borning Light: Poems of Faith

Substantial Evidence
(Haiku Structure)

*The substance of things
hoped for, the evidence of
things not visible (Heb. 11:1)*

Substance can be felt;
evidence requires a sense
beyond retinal.

When you eat this bread
your hands recall the body,
lifted from the cross,

laid warm in the tomb,
the substance of things hoped for –
desperately hoped for.

When you lift the cup
remembering the blood shed –
ruthlessly wrung out –

faith alone ignites
the hope unfathomable;
evidence enough

Spread the Joy!

Merry Christmas!
It rolls from my lips
as easily as
God bless you.

I'm not surprised,
not even offended,
when merchants mute
their "holiday" greetings.

They are for-profit
enterprises; they must
please everyone,
offend no one.

We like it that way;
we all are for-profit
enterprisers; we all
earn our bread that way.

So get off the backs
of the money makers,
let them say it
anyway they wish.

A Borning Light: Poems of Faith

They are not celebrating
the birth of a Savior,
they believe their
profits will save them.

But we who know
the blessed One
who came to bring
us everlasting treasure,

Say, "Merry Christmas!"
We have no axe to grind,
no buck to make, just joy
to share with one and all.

Though You Make Your Bed In Hell

Sentience is the rule of the universe.
The throbbing stars and quarks,
may, in their tongue, converse;
the mute can trace their marks.

The lovely man-made swamp
that lies along the way I go
hides within its foliage, damp
sentiences that ebb and flow.

A Borning Light: Poems of Faith

In woods I loved to trek,
on rocks I used to climb,
my living room, my deck;
in summer's heat or winter's clime,

every sensing creature *speaks*;
beneath the weight of *adam's* sin –
waiting that which sentience seeks –
creation groans to be made whole again.

Sentience is the faithful constant;
all living things and all things living
sense and *speak* – some hesitant,
some bold – but all responding

to the Voice that sent them forth
into the void: "Be fruitful; multiply;
I give you voice; I fix your worth,
and though from me you seek to fly,

and on the farthest star to dwell,
or in the ocean depths to hide,
though you make your weary bed in hell,
I'll seek for you, I hear your cry –
My Love abides."

A Borning Light: Poems of Faith

Unseen Presence
(*Look, I am with you always.* - Jesus)

Eldila inform us of your presence Lord,
coming, as they do, in rainbow radiance,
splashing colors on ceiling, walls and floor,
urging *us* to offer *You* our affiance.

Offer it to you, we do, our unseen Lord.
You ever seek a prism that reveals
to our unseeing eyes the flaming sword
our unseen Lord, in service to us, wields.

Eldila (singular Eldil) In C.S. Lewis'
Out of the Silent Planet

We call the rainbow splashes from a crystal
hanging in our eastern window *Eldila*. They
serve as reminders of God's presence.

A Borning Light: Poems of Faith

Two Poor Rich Men

Luke 12:13-21

The poor will always be with us.
Not because God wills it to be so –
There are, after all, no poor in heaven.
Our Father, who art in heaven . . .
Your will be done . . . on earth,
as it is done in heaven.

God, seeing our world's wretchedness,
sent His Son into the muck;
born in a stable, raised by the poor,
eating and drinking with outcasts
and sinners, wandering homeless,
dying deserted . . . on a cross.

His Spirit still inhabits the haunts
of the outcast, the downtrodden poor.
You imagine Him standing in awe
before the gleaming shrines we've raised,
in ignorance, to bear His name.
But look, he eats and drinks with sinners.

How different the world would look
if no church had ever cast its shadow

over the hovels of the hungry;
if instead, believer's worshiped,
like their Lord, in homes with the poor,
the hungry, the naked, and the sick.

How different our world would be
if, in imitation of their Lord,
believers refused to be rich
until none they knew were poor –
until the will of God was done
on earth as it is in heaven.

The parable does not condemn
the rich farmer for efficiency,
does not imply that he should
cease to reap abundant harvests;
it only damns the barns he built
to hoard the precious grain.

Mark 10:17-22

A poor man said to a rich man,
". . . sell all your possessions
and give the money to the poor;
then follow me, and you will be rich."
Unwilling to be wealthy,
the poor man sadly walked away.

A Borning Light: Poems of Faith

To Everything A Season
Poems Celebrating Nature

I live where there are seasons, four of them, each distinct most years. There are those who loath one season or another but I've seldom heard Spring and Fall maligned. Spring is the harbinger of better things to come after a long and arduous Winter. Fall, while it cannot erase the thought that Winter is returning, nonetheless wows us with it autumnal display of beauty.

Each season serves a special purpose. Even winter, especially the harshest winters, serve to kill off blights and insects that would otherwise run off with the earth. And I'm told that those long sub-zero days perform a service in incubating in their cold certain seeds that would not sprout without having endured that trial by ice.

So the wisdom of our Maker is displayed in ways that often vex us. If it is vexing enough, most of us have the option of going to some part of the country or the globe that suits us better than Wisconsin.

To Everything A Season: Poems Celebrating Nature

I have no intention of moving . . . unless it would be to northern Wisconsin where I understand the snow sometimes reaches a depth of four or five feet.

To Everything A Season: Poems Celebrating Nature

A Rainy July Morning
(A Haiku Trio)

You do all things well.
I'd rather watch Your rainfall
trace a window scene

than be a *drudge*, spell-
bound; a mental slave, enthrall
to a T.V. screen.

You do all things well;
Your faithful raindrops all
rush to make the scene.

A Cold Assize

Autumn air
awaits the day's arising,
taunting Geos as she tries to rouse
her stiff arthritic bones.
Even fiery Sol, with aching groans,
awakes with tentative apprizing.

To Everything A Season: Poems Celebrating Nature

Geos, scrounging,
seeks for something warm
to wrap her aged, shivering body in;
brews some "warm" and slowly takes it in,
and gazing through the haze sees
Autumn charm.

An Ode To A Beautiful Wood

Where I live a woodland path goes by
And I have often walked down it to spy
The wonders buried deep within the breast
Of woods I guard the entrance to, lest
Some rude soul should stumble in and desecrate
The beauty that I've found beyond her "gate";
Someone who'd care not for her sacredness;
Who does not know her blessedness.

I've learned to know her secret places,
All her shades and moods and faces;
I've seen her weep on stormy days
And heard her laugh when sunshine plays
Upon her lap in piles and piles of golden leis.
I've heard her sing her songs in ways
That break the heart of all who hear;
Of all who hold this woodland sister dear.

To Everything A Season: Poems Celebrating Nature

I never visit her but that my heart is filled
With longing to remain until all sound is stilled,
And I can hear the beat of her dear heart,
And feel a oneness with her, part for part,
I never leave but that I long, before I go,
To lay some token on her earthen floor to show –
Or hang some words in space for wind to blow –
And tell her I have passed her way – so she will know.

The Fall Guy

I left the oak leaves lying on the porch so long
the first snowfall cemented them to the decking.
I should claim I waited, fair Autumn to prolong.
Alas, the truth is I was procrastinating.

June 30th in Wisconsin

Time was when Winter was winter
and Summer was summer;
when Spring and Fall would inter-
weave their slimmer
selves between
their larger brothers,
hoping to be seen
as something other;

To Everything A Season: Poems Celebrating Nature

sisters dressed for a ball –
green for sister Springtime,
reds and golds for sister Fall –
each one, one-of-a-kind.

It appears, this year
all are confused;
each seems to bear
their sibling's face bemused.
Is it something we have done
that is causing this confusion?
Is there something to be done
to right the situation?
I want my seasons
to arrive and leave on schedule
and not be given silly reasons
to excuse their breaking rules.

A Haiku For Luna

Quick! See the gold in
the west – slender Luna is
lying on her back

To Everything A Season: Poems Celebrating Nature

spring thaw
(a haiku)

mounds that last week gleamed
in virgin purity show
gritty undersides

A Golden Blossom Frond

He found a little golden flower
That claimed she was a weed,
Meant to grace a field for one brief hour;
Descended from a humble peasant seed.

But he picked her blossom anyway
And took it to his love.
She said his gift had made her day;
That blooms like that are from above.

His friend has sometimes said
That she is merely peasant-made,
But he has chosen her ahead
Of other fronds that fill the glade.

To Everything A Season: Poems Celebrating Nature

April Snowstorm

As quickly as you came, you started melting.
Just as I began to worry how the robins, chirping
in the snow-clad pine, would find their daily bread
you melted, leaving branches bare instead.

Enough's enough, my snowy April friend.
Don't be telling sister May that she should send
another storm to make our pine tree groan
and robins search another place to call their home.

An Overblown Storm

They promised us more,
promised that severe weather
would be coming in.

Just one thunder thump
and a few rain drops are all
they could squeeze from it.

For a storm lover
it was a severe let down,
a teapot tempest.

To Everything A Season: Poems Celebrating Nature

To Everything A Season
(A Haiku)

Summer's end gives fall
a reason – August-ripened
grain is arsenaled.

Jack Frost

It is cold in Wisconsin this week.
The lifted shade revealed that frost
had formed a telltale streak
across the glass – six inch at most.

Jack Frost had been at work,
but Jack had lost his claim to fame;
alas, a feeble pallid smirk
ran artlessly across the thermal pane,

unlike the leafy sunlit marvels
Jack could paint on single panes,
in mansions and in hovels,
in his younger carefree days.

To Everything A Season: Poems Celebrating Nature

Golden Bird

Golden birdie, sing for me,
A song while sitting prettily
Atop a lofty promont'ry.
While I observe admiringly.

Golden birdie, stay nearby;
From branch to branch and in the sky,
Your golden presence from on high,
Flashing down delights my eye.

Golden birdie, distant friend,
I have a hand I'd gladly lend,
For you to perch upon, and then
Our friendship can begin.

Golden birdie, it may be
You'll stay forever in your tree,
But never leave me, birdlessly,
Without the gift of gold I see.

I want a bird who's truly free,
But freely shares her gold with me;
And I will make a pledge that she
Can trust her friend explicitly.

Alphabetical List of Poems

A (Haiku) Gospel Quartet 103
A Borning Light 102
A Business Note 5
A Cold Assize 117
A Day When Stones Cried Out 33
A Golden Blossom Frond 121
A Haiku for Lola 29
A Haiku for Luna 120
A Haiku for Sinners 100
A Long Journey Back to Where We Began –
   Hanging our Thoughts on a Vapor 63
A Rainy July Morning (A Haiku Trio) 117
A Rare Correction 8
A Subtle Word 20
A Two-line Poem 38
Adjectives Are For Poets . . . Uh, Poor Poets 39
Advent of the Promise Drone 9
Aerial Warfare (A Haiku Trio) 76
Against Blind Intolerance of Islam 75
An Author's Dilemma 3
An Easter Haiku 102
An *ism* With A Father's Heart 34
An Ode To A Beautiful Wood 118
An Old Man's Dilemma (A Haiku) 105

An Old-fashioned Christmas Card 32
An Overblown Storm 122
And They Say The Taxes Are Eating Us Alive 79
April Snowstorm 122
Arizona Tragedy (A Haiku Trio) 33
Believe Me, We Are Awash In Anonymity –
   Seven Haiku for Anonymity 72
Body Lovers 24
Bucking the Lord's Day 75
Coupled 23
Doggy Kisses 25
Don't Forget to Send in the Cash 79
Elucidate 12
Extending Love 19
Fall Colors Make Me Believe 105
Firiel 46
Four (or Five) Haiku Proverbs 101
Galadriel 47
Gallup-in In Circles 3
Golden Bird 124
Grieving the Uses of BG 71
Hand-me-down Warfare – A Meditation from a
   Lover of Fireworks 81
He Comes (A Haiku Quartet) 106
Inbreathed (A Haiku) 37
Jack Frost 123
June 30th In Wisconsin 119

Justice, Blind Justice (A Haiku Quartet)	65
kids again (a haiku quartet)	4
Legions of Darkness	44
Let There Be Light (A Haiku Quartet)	88
Making Do With What I have	37
Mikhail Kalashnikov, How Do I Love Thee?	69
Morning in a Fairie Glen	48
No Ordinary Cloth	24
No Shame In Going Home	106
Not News	12
Oh Shucks!	7
Our Final Resting Place (Haiku Musings)	93
Perverting a Good Thing	74
Praying for Nero	80
Responding to an NYT Report	13
résumé	104
Shadows	43
Shared Endeavors – Shared Rewards	22
Sharing A Treat	25
Sharing	23
Should I Join Facebook?	86
Shredding (1952 – 2014)	94
Simple Faith (A Haiku)	103
Single Snowflake Threatens Millions	11
Sliding Into Heaven	13
Son-time on a Rainy Day: November 6, 2013	19
Spider Lives	77

Spread the Joy	108
spring thaw (a haiku)	121
Standing Watch: Questions for an Ancient Tree In a Chicago Park	67
Substantial Evidence (Haiku Structure)	107
Sun-dappled Days	58
Sunday Afternoons of Old	29
Thank God for Words	85
That You Are There	21
The Fall Guy	119
The High Price of Ageing (A Haiku Lament)	92
The Human Malady	66
The Hurt and the Hurter (A Haiku Meditation)	87
The Prophet in the Wilderness – Marilynne Robinson	61
The Righting of the Costa Concordia	73
The Serpent in Eden (A Haiku Quartet)	99
The Value of a Dream	48
Things Missed and Things Missed	90
This Day (A Haiku)	100
Though You Make Your Bed In Hell	109
To Everything A Season	123
To Fairie and Back on a Foggy Morning	48
Too Much Self-examination	8
Touched by An Angel In A Shirt Too Small	5
Treasures in Earthen Vessels	99
Two Poor Rich Men	112
Unseen Presence	111

Vegewels	7
Watching an Old Man Outlive His Wisdom	61
We're (Not) Using Our Heads	14
Week-end Fare	63
What is the Cost of a Burger	89
When I am Gone	38
Who Is My Friend?	90
Working The Night Shift	15
Wrecking Your Chances	39
Your Presence (A Haiku Trio)	100
Your You-ness	21
zephered	4

About the Author

Jim Rapp is a retired public school teacher.

Previous to his 27-year teaching career he served as pastor of a congregation in River Falls, Wisconsin for six years. In his retirement years he served his church in Eau Claire, Wisconsin as Director of Drama for 12 years until May 2009.

Jim holds a Diploma in Theology from North Central Bible College (now North Central University) 1958, and a Master's Degree in History with his major area of interest being the Ancient Near East from University of Wisconsin-River Falls 1971.

He has written six dramas, five of which have been staged. In his twelve years as Director of Drama he co-directed, with Music Director, Cheryl Brandt, twenty-two adult musical dramas and nine children's musicals.

Jim is author of five books of poetry, *Perfect Imperfection; Sandals: The Journey of Abraham and Sarah and Hagar; Second Crop: More Poems by Jim Rapp; Etcetera:An Eclectic Expression of Humors* and *Chips*. He is also author of *Inga & Olaf: Modern Parables*; *Sermon on the Mount: Brief Meditations* and *7 Royalty-free Christian Drama Scripts*.

www.ingramcontent.com/pod-product-compliance
Lightning Source LLC
Chambersburg PA
CBHW061326040426
42444CB00011B/2797